Twelv
of Highly Successful Traders

Ruth Barrons Roosevelt

Traders Press, Inc.®

Copyright© June 2001 by Ruth Barrons Roosevelt. All rights reserved. Printed in the United States of America. No part of this publication may be reproduced, stored in a retrieval system, or transmitted, in any form or by any means—electronic, mechanical, photocopying, recording, or otherwise—without the prior written permission of the publisher.

ISBN: 978-1519587480

Published by
TRADERS PRESS, INC.®

Revised Edition 2013

Barrons Books

I would like to dedicate this book to all Traders everywhere who choose to improve.

IF YOU ARE NOT COMPLETELY
SATISFIED WITH YOUR MINDSET FOR
TRADING. GIVE ME A CALL·

Peak Performance Coaching Program

Consider entering my personalized coaching program. This is a powerful, proven, winning program. I personally work with a select number of traders to individually assist them in becoming consistently profitable. Before you can control your trading, you need to control yourself. I help you do just that. My system for self-management will assist you to be clear minded, calm, focused and able to take right and timely action in the markets.

Call me to determine whether or not this program is for you. The openings are limited, so I reserve the right to accept only those traders who are committed to trading excellence. Call me now, but only call if you are prepared to make powerful changes in your life and your trading. What would happen if you turned your past mistakes and weaknesses into stepping stones and became a consistent and disciplined trader?

WORKSHOPS AND SEMINARS

From time to time I conduct weekend workshops and seminars on the psychology of successful trading. Because we use state of the art techniques for mental change, these workshops are truly transformational. Call me to see where and when my next seminar will be.

Ruth Barrons Roosevelt
1-800-692-0080
RuthRoosevelt.com

POWER TRADING FOR POWER PROFITS
A Home Study Audio Course

Power Trading is a complete system for managing your mind to make money. This audio course will teach you to overcome trading hesitation, stay with winning trades, cut your losses before they hurt you, trade with confidence, and get off the emotional roller coaster.

I teach you how to consciously run your mind while you trade, and through the use of self-hypnosis tapes you also learn unconscious associations that guide you to think like a winner. It can make the difference between failure and success or mere survival and triumph.

> *Ruth Barrons Roosevelt, J.D.*
> *165 William Street*
> *NY, NY 10038*
> *1-800-692-0080*
> *http://www.RuthRoosevelt.com*

Twele Habitudes of Highly Successful Traders

Table of Contents
Contents

Introduction   *1*

Chapter 1   The Habitude of Preparedness............ 11
Preparing Your Mind and Psyche for Trading. Prepare Your Strategy. Prepare a Money Management Plan. Gather Sufficient Capital to Trade. Commitment. Arrange to Have Data and Information. Set Goals: A Sure Fire Method.

Chapter 2   The Habitude of Detachment..............19
The Issue of Identification. Focus on the Process of Trading. Draw A Boundary. Viewing from Perceptual Positions. Keep Your Ego Out of Trading. An Anxiety Cure.

Chapter 3   The Habitude of Willingness to Accept Loss.. 29
Simple Cost of Doing Business. Not Your Job. Winners Expect to Win. The Impasse. Growing Losses. A Story of Terrible Trading. Hard Wired to Not Cut Losses and Let Profits Run. Resistance. Overcoming Resistance. Feedback Not Failure.

Chapter 4 The Habitude of Taking Controlled Risk 39
The Risk Taker. The Odds. Life Style Tendency and Preference. Excitement or Fear. Control. Individual Differences.

Chapter 5 The Habitude of Thinking in Probabilities 47
All We Have. Scientific Enhancement of Probabilities. Self-Doubt and Self-Importance A Distortion of Probabilities. Probabilities Keep You Out of Trouble.

Chapter 6 The Habitude of Being Comfortable With Uncertainly 53
A Rich Opportunity in the Unknowable. The Benefits of Uncertainty. The Need To Be Right. A Story. The Open Mind. Asking the Right Questions.

Chapter 7 The Habitude of Taking of Bong Term View 63
Balance and Equanimity. Don't Sweat the Small Stuff. Stop Doing What Doesn't Work. Viewing Drawdowns as Temporary. Gaining Clarity. An Elusive Concept That Serves You.

Chapter 8 The Habitude of Abundance Consciousness 69
A Choice Between Scarcity Or Abundance. The Power To Overcome Setbacks. How Scarcity Effects Trading. Breaking the Profit Ceiling. Valuing Wealth. Affirm and Focus on Abundance

Chapter 9 The Habitude of Optimism 75
Explanatory Style. Optimistic Traders. Pessimistic Traders. Realistic in the Present. The Meaning We Give to Events. EEC.

Chapter 10 The Habitude of Open Mindedness and Clarity of Thought and Perception.. 85
The Problem of Bias. A Matter of Identity. Bias in Trading Equals Danger. Some Words as Clues. Indicators as Lie Detectors.

Chapter 11 The Habitude of Courage 91
Practicing Courage. Courageous Questions. Respect: Not Recklessness. The Hero's Journey.

Chapter 12 The Habitude of Discipline 99
Education and Control of the Self. Trading With Integrity. Doing Not Trying. Acting In Support of Trading Goals. Specific Trading Guidelines. Trading As An Art and Adventure. Balance.

Introduction

THE HABITUDES

"Character is simply habit long continued."
—Plutarch

"Nothing is stronger than habit."
—Ovid

Have you ever found yourself fully intending to do one thing and ending up doing quite the opposite? Or promising yourself you won't do something and going ahead and doing it anyway? Or wanting to do something but finding yourself not doing it? These are the sins of omission and commission and mixed behavior.

I see it all the time. A trader has a special set of guidelines for trading that works for him for months until one day he violates all his rules and loses a year's earnings. A day trader goes into the market to take a point profit out of a stock and ends up trapped in 32 points of loss. A professional bond trader puts on a speculative position in his own account and leaves it moving against him for a year until he's lost $200,000 and his own self-respect. Still another trader starts out each day determined to trade and finds herself sitting immobilized in front of her computer for months on end, nothing ventured, nothing gained. And so forth. The human condition is at work trading.

Successful traders, on the other hand, approach trading with a supportive mindset. Their attitudes toward key aspects of trading work for them. These attitudes are so consistently held that they become habitual patterns of thought and action.

When an attitude becomes a habit, we could call it a *habitude*. An attitude that has become habitual, then, is a *habitude*.

For most traders these attitudes don't come naturally. They need to be learned, developed and maintained until they do become habitual. This book will explore effective attitudes toward trading and show how each attitudinal shift enhances the other attitudes. When these attitudes become your habitudes for trading, you will have developed a mind power for trading.

"Habit is a sort of second nature."
—Cicero

Habitude One

A successful trader has a commitment to trading and comes **prepared** to trade. Methods are verified. Homework is completed. Precaution is taken and things are checked out. She is prepared strategically, emotionally, and financially.

Habitude Two

A successful trader is **detached** from the results. He thinks in terms of process and believes in the validity of the process. He understands that he is more than the trading. He does not tie a fragile ego to any day's trading results. He has faith that over time he will make money. Therefore, the results of any one trade are statistically unimportant. He thinks in terms of probabilities. A single trade says nothing about the trader himself.

Habitude Three

A successful trader is **willing to accept loss.** She understands that losing is an integral part of the trading process. She knows and accepts on a deep level that individual losses and losing periods must occur as they are an endemic part of trading. She doesn't like loss. She doesn't expect to lose. She simply accepts loss as a cost of doing the business of trading.

Habitude Four

A successful trader is **at ease with controlled risk.** He is a risk taker. He is willing to risk in order to win. He is courageous: he'll take a chance. He manages risk to his comfort level. And very frequently that comfort level tolerates substantial risk. He may even find risk exhilarating. It keeps him on his toes, keeps him alert and at the top of his game.

Habitude Five

A successful trader **thinks in terms of probabilities.** While she may have certain biases in her life, when it comes to trading, she realizes she does not know. All she has are probabilities. And probabilities are enough. She puts herself in alignment with the probabilities. Probabilities are at the core of her trading decisions. Through consistent application of the probabilities, she increases the likelihood of winning.

Habitude Six

A successful trader is **comfortable with uncertainty.** He realizes the future is not knowable and accepts the fact that he only has probabilities, no certainties. In trading, there is no such thing as a sure thing. A competent trader has no particular need to be right. He understands that being right or perfect has no place in trading. Therefore, he's flexible. He's willing to change his mind. He's alert to scenario changes. He accepts market information that tells him whether he's on the right track or the wrong track.

Habitude Seven

A successful trader takes the **long term view.** She is willing to lose in the short term. She understands that losses are a necessary cost of doing business, much like inventory is to a merchant. Drawdowns are viewed as temporary. She realizes that individual wins or winning periods are also only a part of a much broader process. Each trade is but one of a string of trades. She sees trading as a process that extends over time. What is happening right now is but one piece of a much larger puzzle. Because of this there is no reason to get overly euphoric or despondent.

Habitude Eight

A successful trader has an **attitude of abundance.** Scarcity has nothing to do with his worldview. He affirms the abundance of the universe. He knows he cannot begin to count the stars. He realizes the ocean doesn't care whether you go to it with a bucket or a teaspoon. He sees the market as providing a river of opportunities. Because of this, he knows he can always recover from any setback. He freely uses his money for those things and people he cares about. He builds his equity, and he lets the money flow. He invests in himself and his trading capabilities. The more he makes, the more he gives to worthy causes; and the more he gives, the more he makes. He expects and creates plenty of substance and opportunity.

Habitude Nine

A successful trader is **optimistic.** She is realistic in the present and optimistic about the future of her trading. Because she is optimistic about the future, she can afford to be truthful about the now. There is no need to make up stories about the good or bad things that occurred in the past or are happening now. She takes a clear look at current information. She admits when something isn't working. She recognizes her mistakes and learns from them. Her optimism gives her faith and courage. It keeps her from falling prey to fear and blame.

Habitude Ten

A successful trader has an attitude of open-mindedness **and clarity of thought and perception.** He is aware of his natural biases and takes steps to protect himself from them. He is flexible in response to changing events and changing perceptions. He is willing to listen to the market and is sensitive to the market's changing moods. He knows that if he hears himself saying, "I don't believe this," he'd better believe it and act upon it. He has an attitude of anything can happen, and I can handle anything that does happen.

Habitude Eleven

A successful trader has an attitude of **courage.** She's willing to act in the face of uncertainty and possible loss. It isn't that she knows no fear: she feels the fear and acts anyway. You don't need courage if there isn't some trepidation. As John Wayne **said, *"Courage is being scared to death and saddling up anyway."*** She doesn't take reckless chances, but she does act promptly in accordance with her methodology and market action. She respects the power of the market forces. She respects her capital, her indicators, market data, her live orders. She has a healthy respect, and she balances that respect with her courage. She is on a hero's journey.

Habitude Twelve

A successful trader is **disciplined.** Discipline is putting into action those behaviors which need to be done to get you to your goals. He does what he intends to do, and he intends to win through consistent right action. His actions support his goals. His goal is to make money trading. Therefore, he is patient waiting for trades to set up and mature. He's decisive: he decides easily and acts promptly on the decision. He acts in the right way, at the right time, right on time. And when there's nothing to be done, he waits.

Summary

Each of these habitudes overlaps with the other habitudes to create a personal style of trading. Together these habitudes create a mind set for profitability. Each habitude is separate and discreet, and at the same time it is a seamless part of the whole. You'll notice in my discussion of each habitude, I will often invoke and refer to other habitudes.

> *"How use doth breed a habit in a man!"*
> —William Shakespeare

If any one of these habits of thought is missing from your approach to trading, you could be sabotaging your results. Don't become discouraged. Patterns of thought can be changed. I know. I work each day with traders to assist them in attitudinal shifts so that they can become and remain profitable. I have created audio self-hypnosis tapes to facilitate a trader in changing individual patterns of thought about trading, and to assist in developing new habits and attitudes. My book, *Exceptional Trading: The Mind Game* outlines many state of the art techniques for developing a winning mind set. Your mind is your power, and you can change your mind.

Self Test on the Habitudes

Score yourself from 1 to 10 on the twelve habitudes. Let 10 be the strongest and 1 the weakest. Mark it in your trading notebook that you'll keep through this book and beyond. By assessing your tendencies, you'll know where to concentrate your change work. Remember, one missing habitude could endanger the whole project.

1. Habitude of Preparedness
2. Habitude of Detachment
3. Habitude of Willingness to Accept Loss
4. Habitude of Being at Ease With Controlled Risk
5. Habitude of Thinking in Probabilities
6. Habitude of Being Comfortable With Uncertainty
7. Habitude of Taking the Long Term View
8. Habitude of Thinking in Terms of Abundance\
9. Habitude of Optimism
10. Habitude of Open Mindedness and Clarity
11. Habitude of Courage
12. Habitude of Discipline.

Chapter 1

The Habitude of Preparedness

"To be prepared for war is one of the most effectual means of preserving peace."
—**George Washington**

Preparedness is an essential precondition for any profession, whether it be medicine, the military, professional sports, or even carpentry. Readiness, training, and the appropriate tools are essential. We know what military preparedness involves. A professional athlete would never think of going into a game without extensive training and practice. You don't expect a carpenter to come to your home without a hammer, a saw, and know how. Trading is no exception to the need for readiness.

Successful traders have a habit of being fully prepared. They come prepared psychologically, strategically, and financially to trade. They have an attitude of full commitment to preparation for trading success.

PREPARING YOUR MIND AND PSYCHE FOR TRADING

You need to come to trading psychologically prepared to trade. Your own personality is the multiplier effect of your trading results. **Your strategy, plus**

your money management, plus your capital, multiplied by YOU equals results.

Strangely enough, this is the last place most traders think they need to prepare. They simply assume they have what it takes to enter into this arena and excel. How surprised they are when they find themselves doing things they said they'd never do and not doing the things they said they would surely do. And even when they realize that they are the cause of their failure, they are reluctant to get help.

I have talked with many traders who are sabotaging their trading results. Some can't pull the trigger and sit there day after day doing nothing but watch and marvel. Some are unwilling to take a loss and will let loss after loss eat up their trading account until the pain of keeping that loss is greater than the pain of taking that loss. Some get in trouble by not following their trading rules. Others can't consistently follow a trading system and find themselves skipping the big winners and taking the losers.

And yet, while they may call me to find out about my coaching, they delay signing up for mental training. If I call them back a year later, they're still repeating the same behavior and still reluctant to pay for coaching. "I should be able to handle this myself." they say. But they can't, and they don't. It's the winners who seek assistance for their trading weaknesses. And it's the winners who correct their trading foibles by strengthening their weaknesses and their strengths.

You need to psychologically prepare yourself to execute your plan. Trading requires a mental toughness. Trading demands a mindset that may not come naturally. You cannot charm the market. You cannot persuade the market. You cannot bully the market. You cannot cheat the market. You cannot *merely* study or research the market. You have to TRADE what the market gives you.

A successful trader trains his mind for high power trading. If he needs a coach or mentor, he gets one. He takes the time for meditation, self-suggestion, and positive visualization. He learns helpful questions to ask himself. He does whatever it takes to prepare himself mentally to trade.

Prepare Your Strategy

You need to come to trading strategically prepared. You have to have a plan for putting the probabilities in your favor. You need to know what to do, how to do it and when to do it. I'm continually amazed at how many traders have no written plan. Discover what works. Make certain yourself that it does work. These are preconditions to trading.

George kept losing more than he was making trading stocks. When I asked him what his guidelines for buying a stock were, it seemed he had none. It seemed his decisions were made simply from what others in a chat room were doing. His decisions were simply impulsive and random, and it wasn't working. He needed to create a viable entry and exit strategy, and he did.

A successful trader takes precaution; that is, he is cautious before he begins. He has taken the time to study the situation and to explore the probabilities that will lead to success. He doesn't just shoot from the hip willy nilly. He has written down his guidelines for entering and exiting trades. He knows what his risk is, and he knows when to say that a trade is complete. He knows when to reenter and when to add to a trade. He has rules for telling himself whether a market is trending and what that trend is.

The successful trader understands the dangers of huck-sterism and doesn't just buy any old system that claims to produce 3,000% profit in the last year. He makes certain that real time forward trading has produced the acclaimed results: he doesn't accept the validity of computerized curve fitted back trading.

He realizes that any method or system will have its ups and downs, and he decides in advance what would have to happen for him to change methods. The drawdown would have to exceed historical drawdowns by x percent, or the troughs of the drawdowns would have to come with unprecedented frequency, or the losing period would have way outlasted past losing periods. The winning trader would know in advance when he would step aside and when he would resume trading the method.

If he trades from intuition and discretion, he still has indicators and conditions that must line up before he enters or exits a trade. He checks out his hunches against his indicators.

Prepare a Money Management Plan

You need to **prepare a solid money management or position sizing approach.** How much of your money will you risk on any one idea? When will you add to a winning position?

When will you start taking money off the table? How much will you risk in order to make how much?

Gather Sufficient Capital to Trade

It takes money to trade. You can't start with a paltry sum and expect it to last. You can't expect to get lucky on your first few trades.

> *"For which of you, intending to build a tower, sitteth not down first, and counteth the cost, whether he have sufficient to finish it?"* —Bible: St. Luke

The winning trader is prepared with sufficient capital. He understands that he can't trade on a shoe string. He has decided in advance how much he needs and how much he's willing to risk. Risk capital is money that you can lose and still maintain your life-style and still maintain your peace of mind. He doesn't start trading with capital he needs to live on.

Commitment

The winning trader has made a commitment to the process of effective trading. It's not a random bet or two. He has laid down the foundations for success. This profession demands training, groundwork, practice, and readiness.

This does not mean that you should over prepare, or strive for a perfection that does not and cannot exist. That's research, not trading. As soon as you have something that puts the probabilities strongly in your favor, you're ready to begin. You don't want to begin too soon, and you don't want to begin too late.

You don't want to fall into the trap that Jason, a retired engineer, found himself in. He practiced simulated trading in financial futures for five years. He took over 80,000 simulated trades. His trading was profitable on paper, but he never made any actual money because he never put on a real trade. Every day he planned to, but he never did. In the meantime the money in his account dwindled because of his living expenses. By the time I spoke with him, he had barely enough to trade, and he really couldn't risk it. He had been able to trade before he started his extensive research, but he researched too long and lost the ability to act.

> *"Sow an act, and you reap a habit. Sow a habit, and you reap a character. Sow a character, and you reap a destiny."*
> —Charles Reade

Arrange to Have Data and Information

You need to **prepare yourself with timely and reliable data and information.** If you are day trading, you need instant data, not delayed. If you're position trading, end of the day data will do. Make sure you have all the information you need and have it when you need it. You're trading to make money. Don't stint on the costs of data and information. It will show up on your bottom line.

Stack the probabilities in your favor. Get a strategic and mental edge. Take precaution and be prepared.

Decide what you want from your trading. Figure out what steps need to be taken to get there. What resources will you need? What training will you need? Be willing to pay the price. Remember, **commitment is the beginning of all great results.**

Set Goals: A Sure Fire Method

"We're playing our mind games... Creating the future, out of the now..."
—John Lennon in his song "Mind Games."

First, **put your goal into words.** Form a sentence that is specific, simple, short, positive, in the present tense, and possible. S.S.S.P.P.P. (No, not S&P)

> **S.** Say **specifically** what you want. "I take every signal my system offers me." S. Keep it **simple.** "I trade with courage." S· Make it **short.** "I trust my methods." P. Word it **positively.** "I always use stops." Not "I stop getting stuck in trades." **P.** Say it in the **present tense** because the future is

always a distance away, and the past you can't do anything about. "I make money trading." Not "I will make money trading." P. Choose something that is **possible** and achievable. "I follow my system."

Second, make a **mental movie** of yourself with the goal achieved.

Third, step into the movie and **live it and feel it as if it is *already* true.**

Fourth, **design the steps necessary** to take to get to the goal.

Fifth, **commit** yourself to doing the steps and make a **timetable** to do them.

> ***"Take care to get what you like or you will be forced to like what you get."***
> —George Bernard Shaw

Chapter 2

The Habitude of Detachment

"Disinterested intellectual curiosity is the lifeblood of real civilization."
—**G. M. Trevelyan**

A trader came to see me who was clearly tense. His demeanor reminded me of the expression "strung tighter than a drum." I inquired what the difficulty was, and he replied, "I've had 28 winning S&P trades in a row." I congratulated him on the feat. He responded, "But what if I have a losing trade?" I remarked that he would have quite a cushion to fall back on. "But I'll lose my self-esteem! If I lose my self-esteem, I'll lose everything!"

This trader had put himself in the untenable position of never having a loss. He'd tied his self-respect to a perfect record. It was only a matter of time, and we both knew it. He needed to change his expectations, and he needed to detach his self-image from his trading. He did.

Detachment from trading results is a subtle emotion. The attitude of a successful trader is not indifference, nor is it intense concern. The attitude of detachment is something like alert and interested unconcern. An aloof interest.

A successful trader cares about results. Of course, she cares whether she is making money. However, she is not overly concerned about the results of any given trade. Furthermore, her well-being and self-esteem are not dependent on the results of any given day's trading. She realizes that she is more than her trading. She has drawn a boundary between her trading results and her sense of self. She is confident in who she is regardless of her trading results.

The Issue of Identification

It's very easy to identify with your trading, to become what you do. You say, "I am a trader." And, of course, you are. But you are a lot of other things as well. If all you are is a trader, then you become intricately involved with how good a trader you are, and your self-esteem can rise and fall with results. You become too connected to the trading.

People often become overly sensitive to the question, "What do you do for a living?" They interpret it as a question that establishes their value, their worth to and in society. They don't hear, "What do you do to make money to live?" No. Instead they hear, "Who are you and how important are you?"

Notice how we often answer the question about what we do with what we are. Instead of saying, "I trade futures." we say, "I *am* a futures trader." This takes it to the level of identity. We become what we do. It's common. "I am a doctor." "I am a dentist." "I am an accountant." "I am an engineer." "I am a full time

Mom." And so forth.

We have become the role, and if we do not inherently value that role, we diminish our self-esteem by answering the question; and we become subject to the opinion of the listener as to the importance of our role.

Personally, I am a trading psychologist, a trading coach, a trader, a professional hypnotist, an artist, and a writer. I feel confident about the value of each of these roles. It does not concern me in the least how you respond to the importance of any of these identifications.

By saying, "I am," I have lifted these activities to the level of identity. I am, of course, more than what I do; and I have even more roles than those I listed.

Those who become completely and solely identified with the roles they play can become depressed and adrift when they cease to perform that role. A mother can become devastated when her children leave home. A corporate employee can become immobilized when downsized. A professional can become depressed upon retiring.

When you become fully and solely identified with a particular role, you can become depressed when it's not going well. A mother becomes deeply discouraged when one of her children is having difficulty or when a relationship with a child becomes strained. A trader goes into the dumps when he's experiencing what will end up to be a temporary drawdown.

If you are not comfortable taking your activities to an identity level, answer and think on a doing level. For example, "I am Tony, an optimistic (or whatever) kind of guy. I play golf to have fun, and I trade to make money."

Because it is natural to identify with our major activity, and since others automatically define us by our profession, most people take their business to an I **am** level. Since this is so, it is vital to believe in the value of what we have chosen to do for a living. We need to feel good about what we do as traders. We need to be proud of our participation.

It's hard to detach from trading results when you're fully identifying with the role, and only that role. So make a list of the other things you do and are. Identify with the whole scope of your being. **You are so much more than your trading.**

Focus on the Process of Trading

Another way to detach from trading results is to focus on the process of trading. Look at trading as a game, a game you're good at. Trading is applying a process to the market. Of course, before you begin that process, you need to confirm that it will lead to success over time.

Then you'll trust that if you follow the process, the probabilities are that you will make money. Place your attention on the process rather than the money. This will enable you to execute with confidence. Your focus and your faith are in the process. The process becomes more important than any intermediate results.

Now faith is not certainty: it's simply faith. Probabilities are only probable: they're not assured. Unfortunately, in trading and investing, probabilities are all we have. We have no certainties. You just have to accept that or get out of the game.

Becoming attached to the results of any given trade can create havoc with the trading. For example, if a trader becomes too attached to the results of a trade, she may fail to take the trade. She may add to a losing trade in an effort to turn it into a winner. She may grab the profit too soon, or overstay her welcome. She may put on too big or too small a position. By becoming too attached to the results, she will allow her personality and hopes and fears to interfere in the process.

DRAW A BOUNDARY

We need to have a **boundary** between ourselves and our trading. We are not our trading. We do our trading.

We need to have a boundary between present trading and past trading. Yesterday's trade has nothing to do with today's trade. Absolutely nothing. Those who confuse yesterday's trading with today's trading inevitably get into trouble.

Now a good boundary is just that. It lets us know where one thing begins and another thing ends. A boundary sets limits. A boundary is not a wall, and it's not merging or becoming one with a trade.

Walls completely separate us from what we've walled off and don't allow us to take in relevant information. Of course, there are times when something is so painful or destructive, we need to construct a wall. And we can, but first we would be wise to see what, if any, lessons we can take from the experience.

There are times when we want to merge with a person or an experience or maybe even the trading. You don't need boundaries when you're bonding with a baby or making love or watching a sunset. There may be times when you don't need boundaries when you're in the zone trading. Most of the time, however, if you merge with a trade, you develop tunnel vision and lose perspective. You become overly attached to the results.

Viewing from Perceptual Positions

"In practical life most thinking takes place in the perception area: how we get to look at things."
—Edward de Bono

One way to detach from the trading results is to develop a different perceptual position. What would I think if I weren't in this trade? What would I think if I were some other trader I know or know about? What would I think if I were a neutral observer, a fair witness? Get out of yourself and look at the trade or the trading from a different point of view.

In our relationships with others and in our relationship with trading, there are three different perspectives we can take. The three perceptual positions are self, other, and neutral observer.

To practice the different perceptual positions, remember a minor dispute you had with somebody in your physical presence. Run it through looking out of your own eyes. Now move into the role of neutral observer and look at it from a position eye level and equidistant between the two of you. Then move into the other person and look at it through their eyes. Go back to neutral observer. End up looking out of your own eyes. Notice how much more understanding you have of the situation.

When we're in the self-position, we're engaged. This is where the juice is. But we may lack perspective.

When we're in the observer position, we're disengaged. We may have more perspective, but we can become like a cold fish.

When we're looking at the situation through the eyes of another, we have more empathy, more understanding. But we may find ourselves playing the role of a doormat or not taking our own needs into account.

Experiment with bringing different perceptual positions to your trading. Try placing a couple of chairs near your trading station. Let one represent a mentor. Let the other represent a neutral observer. Sit in the different chairs literally or in your imagination and look at the trading from those perspectives. It will give you insight and help you detach.

Keep Your Ego Out of Trading

"Of all the traps and pitfalls in life, self-disesteem is the deadliest, and the hardest to overcome; for it is a pit designed and dug by our own hands, summed up in the phrase, 'It's no use—I can't do it'"

—Maxwell Maltz

The ego has no place in trading. An unstable ego will attach itself to anything you do. And trading is no exception. You cannot use the trading arena as an area to prove your worth or your capability. It will just bring your trading and your self-esteem to new lows.

If your ego is getting in the way of your trading, you need to build up your self-esteem. One way to do this is to begin to appreciate yourself. Pay attention to what you're doing that's good. Give yourself recognition for the little things you do as you go through the day. Make lists of your accomplishments. Make lists of your positive attributes. Each day ask yourself, "What did I do today that I'm proud of?" Ask yourself, "In what ways am I improving?"

A secure ego does not need to prove itself. If you're having trouble separating your ego from the trading, read Chapter Eight in my book ***Exceptional Trading: The Mind Game.***

An Anxiety Cure

Anxiety is a forward looking emotion that tells you that there is something in your future for which you need to prepare. Ask yourself, "What can I do to prepare for this?" And do whatever you can.

Then, in your imagination go out into the future to just after the successful conclusion of the event you were worried about. Imagine and visualize the successful conclusion of the event.

Most people do just the opposite of this. They go out into the future in their imagination and picture and feel the unsuccessful conclusion of an occurrence. How many times have you gotten an entry signal and imagined how bad you'll feel when you're stopped out? Don't do this. Imagine instead that the trade goes where the probabilities tell you it will go.

One trader said to me, "But, Ruth, if l imagine making money on a trade, I'll feel so bad when I lose!"

I replied, "Do you want to feel bad both before and after?"

Detach. Detach. Detach. Trading is no be-all and end-all. You are so much more than your trading. Value yourself. Focus on the verified process of your trading over time. Enjoy the process. Play the game. Draw a boundary. Look at it from different perspectives. Imagine your success.

Chapter 3

The Habitude of Willingness to Accept Loss

"Whether I get out at a profit or loss does not matter. "
—Bernard Oppetit

Taking a loss does not make you a loser. This is so important, I'm going to say it again. **Taking a loss does not make you a loser.** In fact, taking a loss can keep you from becoming a loser.

Successful traders accept loss as a simple part of the process of trading. Since loss is an integral part of trading, you have to be willing to accept the inevitability of losing trades. Profits and losses are like night and day, like rain and sunshine, summer and winter, spring and fall. Both profits and losses are natural to trading. By totally accepting the necessity of taking some loss, you ease the intensity of trading.

SIMPLE COST OF DOING BUSINESS

View it as cost of doing business. If you're going to open a grocery store, you can't object to buying food. You can't say, "oh, I hope I don't have to purchase any more groceries this week!" Likewise, if you trade, you can't say, "Oh, I hope I don't have any losses this week!"

A business person hires people to do work for him. This is an expense of the business. Generally speaking, the business person doesn't view the payroll as a net loss to the business but rather as a debit against future profit. A successful trader views losses in the same manner. He expenses losses against profits.

Not Your Job

Many people think that their job as a trader is to choose only winning trades. Since that is impossible, it's a foolish way to look at trading. It sets you up for failure. You cannot hold yourself to the standard of the impossible. I often say to my clients, Write this down. "It's not my job to know whether a trade will be a winner or a loser. It is my job to recognize the signals and act upon them."

I'm not saying that trading is not about winning. Trading is about winning, about winning over time. It's about slowly growing an increasing equity curve, and slowly growing your skills.

Winners Expect to Win

It's also about being a winner. Winners expect to win. Losers expect to lose. You expect to win even as you're willing to have losses.

As a trader you want to think of yourself as a winner. Think of yourself as a winner who does the things that winners do. Winners accept loss.

"Winners and losers are self-determined. But only winners are willing to admit it."

—John Wooden

Trading is about both winning and losing. With a winning mindset you will view trading losses as insignificant and a natural part of the game. You can be a winner even when you're losing. Individual losses and individual draw-down periods happen. That is an undeniable fact.

If you don't like this fact, you might as well get out of the game. There's no way you can trade if you resist any and every loss. You'll only frustrate yourself and your methods. You'll only disappoint yourself. If you really don't want to lose, forgive yourself, and put your money into safe interest bearing instruments. If you're not willing to lose, you may not be able to actually trade. It's a common malady. Let me tell you a story.

The Impasse

It was as if she were all dressed up with nowhere to go. More than anything in the world, Melanie wanted to successfully trade S&P futures. And yet, here she sat, after all the training, after all the courses, day after day, watching the signals go by; and she never put on a trade.

"What's the matter with me?" She'd ask. "Why can't I just put on a trade?"

It was like trying to swim through glue just sitting there in front of the computer. She'd see the opportunities come and go. And she wouldn't do anything. She'd sit frozen like an ice sculpture melting. Then, as the trades went on to make money, she'd feel even worse.

She'd start determined to trade yet feeling at the mercy of the markets. It was as if she were throwing herself into the abyss. Or rowing out into a tumultuous sea in nothing but a small boat.

Day after day after day, she felt demoralizing grief at her inability to act. The protagonist in Melanie wanted to trade. Freedom! "I can support myself trading! I can go anywhere, do anything, buy myself expensive clothes! I can take care of myself!" Freedom shouted.

The antagonist in Melanie stopped her dead in her tracks. Fear! "What if I'm wrong? What if I lose? What if it goes the other way?" Fear would whisper.

Freedom and Fear were doing the shadow dance in Melanie's heart. "Today's the day!" Freedom would proclaim. "It's not safe!" Fear would respond. Push-pull. Advance-retreat. A circular dance.

"What is the worst that could happen?" Freedom would plead. "I can only lose a little bit of money. That's got to be preferable to sitting here stuck."

"What if you really can't do this?" Fear would ask. "You'll lose your dream, and then where will you be?"

Freedom kept Melanie at the computer. Fear kept her inactive. Day after day after day after…nothing.

Growing Losses

Ironically, traders who seek to avoid loss frequently end up losing and often losing big. Some miss opportunity by failing to pull the trigger. Some wait for confirmation only to enter when the trade is mostly over. Some lose because they refuse to recognize a losing situation when they're in it. Some, in a losing trade, will avoid taking that loss only to find it getting bigger and bigger. Only when the pain of holding on to the loss is greater than the pain of getting out of the trade will they get out.

Clearly the quicker you take a loss, the less damage you'll do to yourself both financially and psychologically. Losing trades are like dirty dishes in the sink. You're going to have to take care of them sooner or later, so you might as well do it right away. Once out of a trade, your mind is free to look for new opportunities. And you've stopped tormenting yourself.

The desire not to take a loss is also behind the disastrous policy of adding to a losing trade. The worse it gets, the greater you raise the stakes by putting more money into an untenable situation.

A Story of Terrible Trading

Nicholas Leeson, the trader who brought down the Barings Bank in February, 1995, is a made to order example of the business of not facing up to a loss and getting out. He's also a perfect example of the dangers of adding to a losing position in hopes of digging your way out. The Barings Bank was the bank that lent the United States the money to make the Louisiana Purchase. When Nicholas Leeson finished his trading for the bank, Barings was sold for the equivalent of $1.40.

You remember the story. I analyze it at length in **Exceptional Trading.** Leeson started with a bet that the Nikkei would remain stable at around 19,000. He sold an option straddle. By January 13 he was net long the Nikkei by 3,024 contracts. (Keep in mind that according to the rules of the Simex where he was trading, a person should not be net long or net short more than 1,000 contracts in all contract months combined.)

On January 17, the Kobe earthquake hit and the Nikkei began selling off, gradually at the beginning, and then picking up speed—first breaking 19,000, then 18,000, and finally breaking 17,000 before those left to handle Leeson's mess could liquidate the position.

Leeson had time after the earthquake to get out of the position and manage the loss. He could have reversed the position and gone short. He didn't. He kept adding to his position as the Nikkei went down and down and down. By January 20, he had 7,135 long contracts. By January 27, he was long 16,852 Nikkei contracts. Then, by Friday, February 24, Leeson was long a total of 61,280 Nikkei futures contracts on three exchanges. On top of that he was short 25,900 Japanese government bond futures that were also losing.

As the losses got bigger, the prospect of realizing them became more and more terrifying. In the end he was throwing up in the men's room. Finally, he skipped the country leaving a note saying, "I'm sorry." In just two months of over-trading, of not taking a loss, and of adding to a losing position, Nicholas Leeson single-handedly brought the 233 year old Barings Bank to its knees.

Hard Wired to Not Cut Losses and Let Profits Run

It's a simple rule of trading. We all know it. Cut your losses. Let your profits run. And yet many traders don't. Why? They fear the loss. When they're losing, they don't want to acknowledge they're losing. They *hope* it will go away.

When they're winning, they fear they'll lose their profits. Instead of *anticipating* that the profits will continue to develop, they grab the little they have and let the big money go.

In the one case they hold on with hope, and in the other they jump out with fear. It's almost as if we're hard wired to do the opposite of what we need to do to make money. **We need to think differently when we trade. We need to short circuit losses by accepting and taking them. We need to ride out the winners until our methods tell us the trip is over.**

Nicholas Leeson is an outsized example, to be sure. All of us know times when we or others didn't take that first loss, got stubborn, or sloppy, only to learn one more lesson. I've seen a floor trader in the bond pit lose a week's worth of careful earnings in one careless silver trade where he didn't bother to place a stop. I've seen a currency trader stick with a losing position for over a year! I've seen a dreamy kind of trader not even aware that his $60,000 profit had now turned to a $30,000 loss. I've seen a careful, frugal woman buy Qualcom at $200 and ride it down to $57. I've seen a one lot S&P day trader end up taking home 5 losing S&P contracts. I've seen a trader make a simple error and end up trading that error into an extensive losing position as if it were a trade of immense conviction.

Resistance

It happens. But not to those who easily accept losses as a normal part of the trading game. It's the resistance. Remember: what you resist persists. Refusing to take a loss, refusing to admit the absolutely inevitable, you get what you don't want.

Part of the resistance comes from making an individual trade too important. One trade viewed as but one in a series of trades will not take on such a life and death struggle against loss. Each trade is statistically unimportant.

Part of it comes from thinking that you have to be right. You try to work it out so you can prove yourself right. When you accept the fact that you don't have to always be right about what is basically unknowable, you take a huge burden off yourself. Remember, it's not your job to know, so why should you need to be right?

Part of the struggle comes from tying your self-esteem to a trade. You try to avoid loss to prop up your self-opinion. Respect yourself even when you take losses.

Part of it comes from not focusing on probabilities, but rather focusing on the possibility. Remember probability is much stronger than possibility. You're ready for possibility, but you focus on what is probable. You want to focus on where you expect the trade to go. When you look solely at your risk, you begin to imagine it; and it becomes difficult, if not impossible, to take the trade.

Some of the resistance to taking losses comes from thinking there's a limited supply of money. True your financial resources are finite but your financial possibilities are unlimited. Think positively.

Overcoming Resistance

Resistance can be overcome by changing your thinking. Let me finish the story I told you earlier in the chapter.

Melanie called me and left a message on my answering machine. "This is Freedom! I just dipped into the S&P, and took out five points!"

I laughed with joy when I heard the message. Melanie had learned to imagine probability of success and accept the possibility of loss.

Freedom had learned to ask, "What if this trade's a big winner?"

And that trumped Fear's asking, "What if I lose?"

Feedback Not Failure

We need to look at our trading as we look at any other endeavor in life—that there is no such thing as failure, there is only feedback. We do something and we get results. Results give us information that helps us make another decision and take another action. Living and trading are rich processes filled with give and take. Losses are not failures. They are feedback. And feedback takes us forward.

> *"If you can dream—and not make dreams your master; If you can think—and not make thoughts your aim; If you can meet with Triumph and Disaster And treat those two imposters just the same... Yours is the earth and everything in it. And—what is more—you'll be a man, my son!"*
> **—Rudyard Kipling**

Chapter 4

The Habitude of Taking Controlled Risk

"Since the beginning of recorded history, gambling— the very essence of risk taking—has been a popular pastime and often an addiction...

Human beings have always been infatuated with gambling because it puts us head-to-head against the fates."
—Peter L. Bernstein

THE RISK TAKER

Successful traders are willing to risk in order to have the joy of winning. The joy of winning is far more rewarding than the sting of any little setback. Successful traders enjoy the intensity of risk. To them, risk is exciting, not frightening. It makes life come alive for them.

They are not reckless. They are not gambling in the popular understanding of the term. Their risk is managed and in proportion to their expectation for gain. They know that if they live by the sword, they can die by the sword. (Their metaphor, not mine. I don't like war metaphors for trading.) Still, when the moment comes to step forward and risk, they do it unhesitatingly. They do not shrink from the opportunity. They have an I can do it. It could very well work. attitude. The lines from Eliot's poetry do not apply to them:

> *"I have seen the moment of my greatness flicker, And I have seen the eternal Footman hold my coat, and snicker,*
>
> *And in short, I was afraid."*
> —T. S. Eliot

Not to make a decision is not to exercise choice. To not act upon a decision is to not have made a decision. Successful traders decide and act. They're people of supreme choice. They choose to make money. They choose to risk. They have an appetite to go forward with the risk and the opportunity.

THE ODDS

They do it, though, based on the odds. Probability is the mathematical center of wise risk. **Successful traders risk to win.**

> *"Without numbers, there are no odds and no probabilities; without odds and probabilities, the only way to deal with risk is to appeal to the gods and the fates. Without numbers, risk is wholly a matter of gut."*
> —Peter L. Bernstein[1]

Life Style Tendency and Preference

Risk taking goes beyond trading. It can be a life style tendency and preference. Among my clients are some highly successful day traders. I'm always curious about what they do when they're not trading.

Some go to Atlantic City or Las Vegas to gamble. Others go rock climbing or snow-boarding or skiing. Some go scuba diving or surfing. Others ride motor cycles or race cars. Being on the edge is an important part of their aliveness. Here also they control their risk. They don't take chances where they don't think they can win. They develop their skills, and they only undertake what they think they can do successfully.

Some years ago I was in a supermarket in Laguna Beach, Ca. I saw a large title on Surfer Magazine saying **"THE JOY OF FEAR."** Immediately I thought of the traders I work with. I bought the magazine and even subscribed. The parallels of surfing to trading are uncanny. In the magazine was the following quote:

> *"We must travel in the direction of our fear."*
> — John Berryman

Well, I would add, "We must travel in the direction of our fear *and expect success."* Surfers are a type who relish the dangerous edge and are like those traders who love the action and love to trade. Both need to practice their craft, be in shape, be alert, know what they're doing, and exercise superb control as they work with the phenomenal forces in which they play.

Why would a surfer get in front of a 20 foot wave? Because he thinks he can make it. There are dangers to be sure. That is the challenge. Mark Foo, a champion surfer, was killed in 1995 while surfing. Sometimes even the best don't make it. The same is sometimes true in trading.

Winners expect to win. Losers expect to lose. And both realize their expectations more often than not. We go in the direction of our dominant thoughts, and we bring those thoughts into our reality.

Excitement or Fear

The same shot of adrenaline that creates excitement in some creates fear in others. When you feel that adrenaline pump as you start to trade, do you interpret it as a possibility that something wonderful could happen or as a signal that something awful could happen?

Whether you feel excitement or anxiety or both depends on how you run your imagination. Sure, there's a possibility of loss and there's a probability of profit if you've stacked the probabilities in your favor. For the risk taker and risk manager this uncertainty between small loss or large profit is where the fun lies.

Control

Fear can be a spur to action. Fear creates the fight or flight syndrome. Good judgment and experience tells you what to do and when to do it. You don't leave it just to your emotions. You exercise choice. A good trader takes risks, but he is in control. Control—personal skill—is a vital part of any risk taking action. In interviews with stunt men, the need to be in control comes out clearly.[2]

Successful traders, traders who last, don't take dead-end chances just for the thrill of it. There is a distinction between playing for the excitement and playing to win. The same is true in other forms of stimulation seeking.

> *"This distinction between arousal-seeking which aids and enhances development, and that which stunts it, is the same as the distinction between exploration and violence."*
> **—Michael J. Apter**[3]

We all have a zone of risk taking in which we can perform optimally. It doesn't pay to push it beyond our limits, nor to stay under our limits. Mihaly Csikszentmihalyi calls this flow.

Flow is the state of mind in which a person is totally absorbed in what she's doing. She feels as if she's flowing along with it. Such a state can be intensely gratifying. A person will be able to step up to a spiral of challenges at an optimal rate of change. But these challenges never become too great for the person's knowledge and skill, even as they continue to create interest and response.

An example would be playing tennis with a player who is sufficiently better than you to make you play at the top of your game but not so much better than you to make you feel inadequate.

Individual Differences

Risk makes certain people come alive. Others are risk averse. These are our individual differences. We all have different degrees to which we need, experience, and respond to excitement. The important goal is to balance that risk propensity or aversion so that we can grow and protect our money optimally as we trade.

> *"I think great traders certainly have to have a psychological stability about themselves, but not too much stability, because one has to have a certain flair for risk. It is a fine psychological blend you have got to look for in a trader; the ability to take risk, the ability to have some courage, coupled with stability in the psychological make-up."*
>
> —Pat Arbor[5]

If you tend to over trade or over risk, you need to pull in your frame of safety. You need to establish trading guidelines that will protect you. You need to be alert to your propensity to over risk and step back every time you catch yourself over-extending.

If you tend to avoid risk, you need to expand your frame of safety. You need to slowly add risk to your trading so that you become emotionally inoculated. Decrease your trading size and/or change to a trading vehicle that is less volatile. When this is comfortable, slowly increase size and volatility.

Remember trading should be fun, but trading should also be profitable. Under or over trading does not enhance the equity curve. Find an arena and an approach to trading in which you can trade in a state of flow and profitability.

1. Peter L. Bernstein, *Against The Gods, The Remarkable Story of Risk,* New York: John Wiley & Sons, Inc., 1996
2. S.Piet, "What motivates stunt men" *Motivation and Emotion,* 11 (2) 1987, pp. 195-213
3. Michael J. Apter, *The Dangerous Edge, The Psychology of Excitement,* New York: The Free Press, 1992
4. MihalyCsikszentaihalyi, Flow: *The Psychology of Optimal Experience,* New York: Harper and Row, 1990
5. Alpesh B. Patel, *The Mind of a Trader,* London: FinancialTimes, 1997

Chapter 5

The Habitude of Thinking in Probabilities

"The real trouble with this world of ours is not that it is an unreasonable world, nor even that it is a reasonable one. The commonest kind of trouble is that it is nearly reasonable, but not quite. Life is not an illogicality; yet it is a trap for logicians. It looks just a little more mathematical and regular than it is; its exactitude is obvious, but its inexactitude is hidden; its wildness lies in wait."
—**G. K Chesterton**

The wildness lies in wait. Still we must think in terms of probabilities. Why? Because that is all we have.

All We Have

Oh, we could do remote viewing. We could call on psychics. We could look to astrology. We could call for divine intervention. We could, and some of us do. Our trading is either in the hands of fate, the gods, guesswork, or probabilities. I prefer probabilities. Even if they're not always probable. Not always is the operative word. Patterns occur—but not always. Systems work—but not always. Fundamentals dictate price—but not always.

Relax. If there were an always, the game would be over. There's no such thing as tomorrow's Wall Street Journal today. That's why trading on inside information is a crime. Inside information predicts—but not always. Even the crime is not a sure thing.

What can we do? Accept what we have. Think in terms of probabilities, and act upon them. Let probabilities be enough for you. Go one further—be grateful for them. After all, probabilities *are* probable.

> *"But to us, probability is the very guide of life."*
> —Bishop Butler

Successful traders think in terms of probabilities. They put themselves in alignment with the probabilities. They grade them. Slightly probable. Probably probable. Highly probable. They will risk more on a highly probable trade than on a slightly probable trade. This is where their money management or position sizing comes in.

SCIENTIFIC ENHANCEMENT OF PROBABILITIES

We get very scientific about all this with our new computer driven enhancement of probabilities. Neural networks. Genetic algorithms. Volatility compilations. We use the computer to expand beyond the capacity of a single human mind. And what do we get? Soothing reassurances mathetically born. And what do we really get? More probabilites that are probable—but not always. The wildness lies in wait.

We cannot program the data of the future into a computer, because we do not have that data. We can program the past into the computer and predict the future, but the past is not the future—always. The wildness lies in wait.

We need to accept our limitations and the limitations of our craft and art. We need to get comfortable with approximate predictions and interpretations. We need to go with what currently is, and trust that the probabilities will keep a current move going for a while.

Self-Doubt and Self-Importance a Distortion of Probabilities

Some people see themselves singled out by some perverse force as destined to fail in trading. These people will buy system after system, only to find that when they start to trade the system, it destructs in ways that it never did in the past. Putting aside the thought that the system could have been curve fitted to the past, what can this person make of this?

I have spoken with many thwarted traders who came to believe that they were personally doomed. If they took a trade or traded a method, it would of necessity go against them. To them it seems as if it always has, and by extrapolation—it always will.

What likely is happening to these traders is that their belief about their personal certainty to fail causes them to unconsciously choose those trades or those methods that will not work. This belief causes them to unconsciously filter out the good trades and reliable methods.

The point I want to make here is that if you continue to view your trading through probabilities glasses, through the prism of likelihoods, you will not be able to see yourself isolated by the fates to failure. The belief in probabilities will keep you searching for the key to success. You will sort through probabilities for ways to succeed.

> *"Probable impossibilities are to be preferred to improbable possibilities."*
> —Aristotle

Successful traders know that probabilities are all they have. For these traders probabilities are enough. Probabilities are more than enough. Probabilities mean they will probably succeed. If not now, later. Probabilities are their safety net. Granted, nets have holes, but still they are nets.

PROBABILITIES KEEP YOU OUT OF TROUBLE

Thinking in terms of probabilities keeps traders out of trouble. If you know a trade has a probability to make money, you'll go ahead and put it on in a timely manner. Why would you not? It's *probably* going to make money.

On the other hand, if you know a trade is *only* probable, you'll put in a protective stop loss. Since it's only probable, you're mindful of other possibilities. It could be a losing trade. Therefore, you protect yourself.

Probabilities keep you in a balanced frame of mind. Thinking in probabilities is quite the opposite of thinking in certainties. Remember there are no certainties in trading. By thinking in probabilities, you keep your perceptions cleared to pick up contradictory indicators or information. Perceptual clarity keeps you in touch with current reality. You won't be telling yourself hypnotic stories about what has to happen or is about to happen.

There's no room for self-delusion.

Thinking in probabilities keeps you from tying your ego to a trade. Since any decision is only about probabilities, it's no big deal if you win, and no big deal if you lose. Because your focus is on probabilities, you keep it on the market rather than on yourself. The moment you start viewing the market in relationship to yourself, you get in trouble. First, you distort your vision. You cannot see what is right in front of your nose. Second, you distort your valuation. Your trading becomes too important. When the trading becomes overly important, all kinds of distortions and misdeeds arise. You've started trading to prove your self-worth, and not to make money.

Probabilities are your power. They give you an edge. Without an edge we're simply at the risk of luck. And luck won't last, not without building a bias towards it. You need to create your own luck. You do that by letting probabilities guide your analysis, your trading, and your feelings.

Chapter 6

The Habitude of Being Comfortable With Uncertainly

"He is no wise man who will quit a certainty for an uncertainty."
—Samuel Johnson

And yet we must. The moment we leave a money market or T Bill for a moving market, we have moved from certainty into uncertainty. For some, this is an uncomfortable place to be. Some see it as an unwise place to be.

A RICH OPPORTUNITY IN THE UNKNOWABLE

"Nothing is certain but the unforeseen."
—Proverb

Successful traders realize that within the unknowable, there is a rich opportunity for profit. They understand that the future of any trade is not knowable in advance. They accept that all they have are simple probabilities.

For these traders probabilities are enough. They welcome the uncertainty, walk easily into it, even as they take precautions against having a trade go against them. They always manage the risk by using actual or mental stop loss orders. They limit the risk because they know they don't know.

The Benefits of Uncertainty

Accepting uncertainty makes an important difference in the way you trade. When the outcome of any trade is uncertain, and you fully acknowledge that uncertainty, you will not be blinded by stories or opinions. You understand that so-called gurus and experts don't know the future either. You don't over trade or under trade because there is no reason to under or over invest. You protect yourself against undue risk. You are willing to act in a timely fashion because you understand that you will never have certainty until it is history.

Since the future is unknowable, you fully grasp that it is not your job as a trader to know whether any given trade will be a winner or loser. Realizing this, you relieve yourself of a huge burden. It is your job to recognize your entry and exit signals and act upon them. You feel no need to second-guess yourself because you've created methods that put the probabilities in your favor, and those probabilities will work for you over time.

The Need To Be Right

Some people have an inordinate need to be right. Deep inside they feel that something terrible will happen if they're wrong about something. This can have multiple effects on their trading.

First, such a trader cannot act quickly. She will hesitate before entering a trade and once in she may hesitate to get out because it would prove she was wrong. She's always looking for confirmation because she needs to be right. By the time confirmation comes, however, it's usually too late.

Second, such a trader may be so overcome with the need to be right that she cannot receive information contrary to her position. The market could be screaming turn around—stop and reverse—as she clings for dear life to the original position. If you need to be right, you'll build your case despite the overwhelming evidence to the contrary. And you'll pay the price.

It's a sad state of events when it becomes more important to be right than to curtail a loss. Let me tell you a story about a man who got into trouble trading because of a tormenting need to be right and a refusal to accept that he was wrong.

A Story

"Clint Johnson is on line three," his secretary was saying.

He felt the familiar lump in his throat, a sense of shame and guilt. "Tell him I'll call him back," he said.

Hubert Hunchley was trapped in a nightmare that would not go away. How could he face his clients after losing so much of their money in this last trade? And his own account was down even more than the clients!

He had put on way too large a position.

Yet he'd been so sure.

He was certain of his research. This company was not going to make money. It would be years before it could turn a profit. The short side was the right side. And yet the damn stock kept going up! The idiots on the internet kept telling themselves nonsense about prospects for future earnings.

He'd gone short at 60, and now the stock was at 85. With every point rise, he could feel the tightening around his throat. He couldn't take it off here. It was too late.

He'd called a trading consultant up in New York. She'd said, "Put a protective buy stop above the highs for half the position and another stop 5 points above that for the other half."

He could not, he'd told her. If he did that, he'd just get stopped out before the stock collapsed.

"Do you want me to do it for you?" she'd asked. "Being right is not just getting the fundamentals right. Being right is cutting your losses. Being right is watching the price. Price is reality."

Easy for her to say. Her reputation wasn't on the line. His was. He'd done extensive research and had the courage to invest upon that solid research. "Price is reality." Well, there was more to this company than price. Debt is reality. No earnings is reality. Bad management is reality.

Damn. The stock was 86—86 ½! 87—87 ¼! He undid his tie.

"Price is reality." Indeed. Well, he knew for sure what wasn't reality. Reality was not the drivel the president of the company was spewing over television. He just couldn't. He just wouldn't. It had to go down!

88—88 ½! 89! Okay! He'd put the stops in at 95 and 100. Why was he paying a consultant if he wasn't going to take advice? This was entirely too much stark reality for him.

"George Leon on line 4," his secretary announced. "I can't speak to him now. Tell him I'll get back to him." Hubert Hunchley felt his face flush and his throat constrict. He just could not explain to George, of all people, why he was so certain about this.

As the market closed, the stock eased back a couple of points. Well, that's a relief! He'd do some more research on the company and fax the results to his restive clients.

The next morning Hubert was back in the office burned out after another sleepless night. Richard Brighten had reached him at home and closed his account. "No more discretionary." Richard had said. That was a punch in the gut. Brighten was a respected leader in the community. If he could meet with Brighten face to face he could persuade him, but Brighten had said no. "Just close the account."

The stock was trading up 3 points in the extended market. Well, he'd wait and see how it traded when the market opened. 90—91 ½! 92—93! It was going to hit his stop! Hubert picked up the phone and canceled the 95 stop just in time. Damn! The stock was 96! He'd better take out the 100 stop.

"George Leon is on line 2. He says it's important."

"I'll be right with him. Tell him to wait." Hubert said. He felt sick to his stomach. Quickly he canceled the stop. He dreaded the conversation, but he couldn't put George off another day.

"George, I know I'm right on this. If we get out here, it'll just turn around. Did you read the fax I sent you?"

"George, please trust me. This company's a piece of shit."

"I know. I know. It's real money you're losing. It'll turn around. It has to. You'll see. We'll make it back on this trade or another one."

"Thanks, George. Yeah, I'll watch it real close."

How could he not? 97—98—99—101! Hubert couldn't believe it. He knew he was right, but he was losing too much money. The humiliation, the ache of being wrong, the pain of losing was just too much.

Finally, Hubert unraveled the position at 1O5, 106, and 107. Only when the agony of losing became greater than the humiliation of being wrong was Hubert able to get out of the trade. Once out of the trade, he didn't feel much relief—only remorse and the thought of what might have been.

Maybe he should buy some puts on the stock just in case the world came back to its senses. And that is just what Hubert Hunchley did.

The Open Mind

Since the successful trader has no particular need to be right, she can keep an open mind to the information that the market gives her. She won't pit herself against the market. She can want what the market wants and go with the flow. She can accept the inherent lightness of the market. For a trader who wants to win (as against be right), price is reality.

Asking the Right Questions

To stay on track there are certain questions you can ask yourself as you trade. Questions are very important because they direct the focus of our minds. Therefore, it makes sense to ask those questions that will take us where we want to go.

Because the market direction is uncertain, you don't ask yourself unanswerable questions such as, "Will this trade be a winner?" "Will the market go up or down?" Instead you might ask yourself the following questions:

"How much could I probably make?" (This gets you thinking about the potential for profit.)

"What is my risk?" (Only after establishing a potential for gain do you turn your thoughts to the possibility for loss.)

"What will have to happen to tell me I am wrong?" (This keeps you alert and on the outlook for contrary indicators even as it keeps your hand steady on the trade as you let your profits develop.)

There are many questions to ask. Consider the following:

"What is the market showing me now?" "What does the market want?"

"Is there anything I'm not seeing, anything I'm missing?"

"What are the probabilities?"

"Am I asking the right questions?"

"What is the significant question I should be asking now?"

Such questions will keep your mind alert to unfolding market conditions, to developing reality. Such questions accept the underlying truth that market movement is uncertain and know-able only in degrees of probability.

The future is not knowable. A successful trader fully accepts the uncertainty and even enjoys the mystery. Herein lies the art and the excitement of trading. After all, if we could know for certain, the game would be over.

Chapter 7

The Habitude of Taking of Bong Term View

"Time is the great physician."
—**Benjamin Disraeli**

As we grow older, we begin to get a perspective on events and things. A baby will collapse into tears, totally distraught over some little thing. For the baby, survival is implied in getting what they want or need right now. Adults see a broader picture. Unfortunately, some traders tend to take a baby's point of view to trading. Each trade, each tick, becomes all important in the moment. Each trade becomes endowed with the significance of survival.

BALANCE AND EQUANIMITY

By taking the long view, a trader keeps herself from being caught up in euphoria or despair or panic. We all know what these emotions can do to a trader. The long view gives you balance and equanimity. The long view gives you wisdom. And wisdom takes away the immediacy of each trade which is just one step in the long journey of trading.

The successful trader views each trade as but one in a series of possibilities and probabilities. As Tom

Basso puts it, "Each trade is but the first of the next 1,000 trades." When this is true for you, each trade is relatively meaningless. A loss? So what, the next one could be a profit. A profit? Well, that's nice, but the next one could easily be a loss. The order of the profits and losses doesn't matter.

Don't Sweat the Small Stuff

When you take the long view, you don't sweat the small stuff. If you get all hot and bothered about something during the trading day, ask yourself, "How important will this be tomorrow or next week or next month?"

Did you get a bad fill? Look at your fills as a whole. If they're usually fair, keep going. The next fill will be better. If they're usually terrible, you need to change the way you execute or you need to change your broker. **Taking the long view also means that you don't keep doing what doesn't serve you.**

Stop Doing What Doesn't Work

Skipping trades, overtrading, bad fills, slow data and so forth when projected over time spell disaster. Traders who take the long view come to terms with what is not working. They don't keep on doing what doesn't work.

Is it a problem with your own mind set? You need to find a way to change this. Get a coach. Do effective mental rehearsal. Meditate. Create new beliefs that support you. Change mental associations. My book, ***Exceptional Trading: TheMind Game*** will show you how to do this.

Does your strategy for entering and exiting the market work? Analyze your trades in groups of 10 or 20. Look at each group as a whole. Be brutally honest with yourself. Project your past and current trading strategy into the future. What will your trading be like if you keep trading like this? Change what needs to be changed.

Find out what works. Verify that it does work. Then and only then you can trade it. A trader who takes the long view won't rush into trading a new method or system until she has fully checked it out to make sure she truly does have an edge.

VIEWING DRAWDOWNS AS TEMPORARY

When you have a verified trading method that works for the most part, you can be comfortable with setbacks. As you project trading your method into the future, you can anticipate winning over time. Because of this you're willing and able to tolerate losses. You detach from the importance of individual and current results.

Since losses are an integral part of trading, it's important to take them in stride. Losses are a necessary cost of doing business. They are like inventory to a merchant or food to a restaurateur. A restaurateur doesn't whine, "Oh, I hope I don't have to buy food today!" Nor does he complain, "Oh, I had to buy so much food last week!" Of course not. Expenses are planned for and accepted. Losses are an expense of trading. By accepting loss we remove its sting.

Only a loser fears loss. Winners accept it. Fear attracts what we fear. We attract that which we focus on, and we focus on what we fear. "Don't lose," says a trader and sooner or later, usually sooner, that trader creates losses. By taking the long view the concern about losing diminishes. The focus is shifted. The concept of losing loses its magnetism for fear and more loss.

By taking the long view a trader ceases to define herself by today's trading. She and her trading are part of a much larger picture. She creates a boundary between herself and her trading. She creates a boundary between one trade and all the rest of her trading.

The long view allows a trader to view a drawdown as a temporary situation. When a drawdown is only temporary, it loses its power to discourage. By taking the long view, a successful trader can remain optimistic even as he experiences a losing period. He can even get excited because he knows that drawdowns are usually followed by periods of large profits.

When a drawdown is believed to be merely a passing phenomenon, it won't disrupt a trader's faith in his proven methods. A drawdown becomes a simple detour on the road to certain success. It's merely a pause in a winning strategy.

Gaining Clarity

The long view enables a trader to be optimistic about the future even as he remains realistic in the present. With an optimistic view of the future, a trader is able to accept with clarity current market conditions. A clear view of current price action is essential to successful trading.

A successful trader accepts the information the market is giving him even if it goes against his current position. He can even say, "Wow! I was wrong. I was so wrong, I'm reversing my position." By not remaining overly caught up in the moment, he is able to stop and reverse. He doesn't try to fight his way out of a losing position only to dig the hole deeper and lose more. He can remain flexible and take **full** advantage of the turn of events.

An Elusive Concept That Serves You

Time is an elusive concept. It's here today and gone tomorrow. The present becomes past even as it turns into the future. The only place we can act is in the present, but we have the past to teach us and the future to anticipate.

> *"Time present and time past*
> *Are both perhaps present in time future,*
> *And time future contained in time past."*
> —T. S. Eliot

As traders we have the whole range of time to entertain in our minds even as we act in the focused present. The expanded range of time considered enables us to do with clarity what needs to be done right now. How would it affect your trading if you could habitually take an expanded view of it?

Chapter 8

The Habitude of Abundance Consciousness

> **"When big money begins to come, it comes so quickly and in such large amounts, you wonder where it was hiding all those lean years."**
> —Napolean Hill

At the root of many trading problems is a sense of scarcity or a lack of belief in the abundance of wealth and opportunity. With abundance we have more than enough. With scarcity we have barely enough or not enough.

Successful traders have confidence that the markets will provide abundant and recurring opportunity and that they can identify and take advantage of those opportunities.

The same is true in general of people who are successful in life. Successful people believe that life offers a cornucopia of opportunities and that they can identify and take advantage of some of them. For them it's really a matter of selecting which opportunities they will commit to and pursue.

When you have an attitude of plentiful source, you also have a sense of deserving to participate in that plenty. If there were only a limited amount of substance, you could feel greedy or unworthy to take more than a limited amount. When you believe in ever-flowing abundance, you feel free to partake liberally.

A CHOICE BETWEEN SCARCITY OR ABUNDANCE

Do you believe in the limited pie formula, or do you believe in unlimited abundance? Whatever you believe will have an influence on your trading results. Successful traders and entrepreneurs see unlimited opportunity. They expect it. They look for it. They affirm it wherever they see it.

THE POWER TO OVERCOME SETBACKS

A look at successful traders and entrepreneurs also shows that they have been able to survive failure as many times as they have had to. They use failure as feedback. They learn from it and make changes and go on. Many super traders have experienced crushing loss in their early trading years. All of them picked themselves up, and with the sure belief that they could make it back, they did just that.

Confronted with a drawdown, a trader who comes from lack will stop trading or change methods or systems only to junk the new methods or systems at the next drawdown. Of course, I'm not saying a trader should stupidly keep doing what doesn't work. What I am saying is that a trader with a sense of abundance and a verified methodolgy won't crumble under temporary loss because she'll know she's simply passing through a difficult time that will end.

Strangely enough, failure is often a necessary stepping stone to success. Those who are too fearful of failure may never get the success they long for. Fear can lead us not only away from the thing we fear but also away from the thing we seek. Ironically, fear can also lead us directly into the thing we fear. My thesis is that underneath fear of failure is a sense of scarcity. After all, if there isn't enough to go around, you can't afford even temporary failure.

How Scarcity Effects Trading

A sense of scarcity can freeze a trader and keep him from pulling the trigger when he needs to get into or out of a trade. Can keep him from ever trading. Can keep him researching, researching, researching until his time and money run out and he still hasn't traded.

A sense of scarcity is also behind the fear of missing out. When a trader is fearful of missing out, he can over trade in terms of size and frequency. He can jump the gun on a trade or force trades that don't fit his criteria. Enough early or forced trades will ultimately result in loss, thus bringing the very opposite of what the trader intended.

Fear of missing out can cause a trader to throw away good money management principles and trade in excessively large size. Over trading, while occasionally bringing a windfall, will ultimately overtax the account and sometimes lead to financial ruin.

Underlying the fear of missing out is the notion that there are only a limited number of opportunities. Thus, greed is produced. Greed is based on the panicky feeling that there will not be enough. For the truly greedy person, whether the greed is for food or money, there never will be enough. There can't be, because if there is universal scarcity, how can there be enough? Greed is the constant longing for more, better, different.

Have you ever experienced overwhelming remorse for a missed trade or a missed investment? Traders often report that the anxiety and regret of a missed trade is far more painful than a trading loss. At the core of such remorse is the lack of awareness or focus on opportunities yet to come.

A belief in limited resources is also often the cause of a profit ceiling, a wealth cut-off point. I see this with traders who get their accounts up to a certain amount and each time proceed to give it all back. Such traders doubt their worthiness to accumulate wealth. Underneath this thought is the belief that there is not enough to go around. If there is a limited source, what right do they have to have so much? They feel unworthy to have more than what they consider their fair share.

Breaking the Profit Ceiling

One way to avoid such a personalized limit is to find a cause you truly care about. Find something larger than yourself and begin to tithe your trading profits to this cause. The more you make, the more you can give. The more you give, the more you can make. You've made an end run around a lurking sense of unworthiness.

Valuing Wealth

In talking about an abundance consciousness, I'm not talking about easy come, easy go. No. That's the inability to value wealth and let it grow. A spendthrift doesn't honor the accumulation of wealth. Those who divest themselves of their wealth as soon as they get it don't see wealth as something good that they deserve.

We need balance. We need to save money and let money flow. We earn. We save. We spend. We invest. We give. We wisely enjoy our money even as we make it grow.

With a sense of abundance we invest and we risk. We can afford to risk—in a calculated and controlled way—because there is more out there.

There is a need here for balance. It's important to value wealth and value opportunity, not squander them. You don't want to squander and you don't want to grasp. You do want to enjoy wealth and you do want to affirm it.

Affirm and Focus on Abundance

To you the earth yields her fruits and you shall not want if you know how to fill your hands. "
—**Kahlil Gibran**

Nature is abundant. Go out at night and count the stars. You can't. There are so many of them. Go for a walk in the woods. The trees and wild flowers are countless. Walk through any major city and marvel at the wealth manifested in the buildings. Sit down to any meal and delight in the variety and richness. Affirm the natural abundance all around you.

Value opportunity. How? Be alert to it and take advantage of it. Select carefully. Don't reach for opportunities that don't exist and don't grab too much of those that do exist. Don't treat opportunity with indifference or casualness. As a trader, take trading seriously and trade with grateful reverence knowing that the rewards can be even greater than you dreamed.

If, however, you do miss a trade or leave a trade too soon, there's no need to stress over it. Bless it and let it go. Learn from it and vow to do better in the future. After all, there is an abundance of future opportunity waiting for you.

Now, I know it's easy to focus on lack and poverty and homelessness and the genuine suffering in the world and fail to notice that opportunity is all around us waiting to be discovered and utilized.

It's easy to overlook the supply. What one thing do we know about our supply—the markets? They are there and will continue to be there with plenty of movement and possibility. They provide us with unlimited possibility. Pay attention to that. Count on it.

Chapter 9

The Habitude of Optimism

"These success encourages. They can because they think they can."
—**Virgil**

We all have to have a somewhat positive picture about trading or we wouldn't keep trading and would never have gotten into it in the first place. Successful traders maintain an optimistic view of the future of their trading—even while they remain clearly realistic about the present and the past.

How do you think after a setback in your trading? Do you maintain your confidence in your methods and yourself? Do you look for what you have learned and ways to improve? Do you expect things to turn around? Or do you get discouraged? Do you say it can't be done? Do you say you'll never do it?

How do you think after a big win or winning period? Do you expect it to continue? Or do you think it can't last?

Explanatory Style

The way you respond to winning and losing periods will depend largely upon your explanatory style.

How do you explain misfortune? How do you explain good fortune? In short, are you basically optimistic or pessimistic in regards to trading? Martin Seligman has done pioneering work on this subject.1

When a good thing happens to an optimist, he says it's permanent, pervasive, and personal. When a good thing happens to a pessimist, he says it's temporary, specific, and not personal. Conversely, when a bad thing happens to an optimist, she says it's temporary, specific, and not personal. When a bad thing happens to a pessimist, she says it's permanent, pervasive, and personal.

OPTIMISTIC TRADERS

Let's break it down into typical comments. After a large winning trade or series of winning trades, an optimistic trader will say such things as:

"I'm a really good trader." "I've developed a really good system." "I have a good feel for the market." "I've got market savvy." Note these are *all personal* comments taking credit for the good trading.

"Wow! I'm going to make a lot of money." "My system is going to do really well." "Soon I'll be trading even larger as I make more money." These comments suggest that the good fortune will continue, and therefore is *permanent*.

"This method works well with the bonds, but it'll make even more with the currencies." "If I can make money with stocks, I can also make money with stock options." "I can trade futures as well as equities and increase my profit potential." Here the speaker is seeing the good fortune *as pervasive*.

Now when an optimist has one or a series of losing trades, he does just the opposite.

"It had nothing to do with me. It was the broker, the slippage, the market, the times, a defect in the system, etc." In short, the losses were *not personal*.

"The next trade will be a winner." "I'll get another stake, and make it back." "The system's due to have a big winning streak." In this case, the losses are *temporary*.

"I'll do better with the currencies than with the grains. They trend more." "I've lost money in futures, but I can always make money with equities." The speaker sees the situation as *specific* to the areas in which he lost.

The pessimist will think and say just the inverse of the optimist. The difference is summed up by the following poem:

*"One ship drives east, another west
By the selfsame winds that blow. 'Tis
the set of the sails and not the gales,
That tell us the way to go."*

Pessimistic Traders

After a large win or series of winning trades, a pessimistic trader will make comments such as the following: "I just got lucky." "That was a fortunate piece of advice." "Anybody can make money in a trend like that." In short, the good fortune was *impersonal*.

"It won't last." "I'm due for a big loser." "That's a once in a lifetime trade." The winning streak is *impermanent or temporary*.

"Just because I happened to make money in stocks doesn't mean I can do it in futures. Everybody loses in futures." "I can't make money in choppy markets." The good fortune is *specific* to a particular situation.

On the other hand when a pessimist has a losing trade or a drawdown, he will reverse the explanations.

"Why am I such a loser?" "How can I be so blankety blank stupid?" "I'm such a stupid idiot, I don't deserve to win." The losses are definitely *personal*.

"If I keep this up, I'll lose my shirt." "What if I lose all my money?" "I'll never get it right." In short, the losses are *permanent*.

"It just figures. No matter what I do, I lose." "My bad luck follows me wherever I go." "The market's a jungle. They're out to kill you." The misfortune is *pervasive* and follows him wherever he goes.

It's all a matter of explanatory style. What's really important about this is that the meaning we give to an event has more impact upon us than the event itself. Once you have labeled yourself as a personal, permanent, and pervasive loser, you have severely limited your ability to win. Fear of loss follows you. You hesitate too long to grab an opportunity. You jump out of a winning trade only to watch it roar away without you. Then, desperately, you'll jump into an iffy or random trade, only to lose.

On the other hand, if you label yourself as a personal, permanent, and pervasive winner, you will have put yourself into a viable position to find out what works, verify that it works, and do what works in a winning way. You'll have a plan, and you'll execute the plan in a timely fashion.

Realistic in the Present

Because the optimistic trader looks with bright enthusiasm towards the future, she is able to be realistic about what has happened in the past and is happening in the present. On the other hand, a pessimistic trader who has limiting doubts about his future trading, may be unwilling to admit what has happened or is actually occurring.

When you're optimistic about the future, you can easily kick out a losing trade. You're looking forward to the next trade, and the next. If you leave money on the table, you can bless it and let it go. You're looking for the next opportunity. "Where is the next trade?"

you say automatically in response to a closed out trade.

When you're optimistic about the future, you can learn from past mistakes. You can make a clear assessment of your trading without feeling threatened. You can look with unfettered honesty at what is not working and stop doing that. You can note what is working and do more of that. And you're free to test out what might work.

When you're optimistic about the future of your trading, there's no need to tell yourself stories about what is happening or could happen. *Wait and see* is your motto.

The Meaning We Give to Events

One of the most amazing phenomena of life is that it isn't what happens to us, but rather the meaning we give to what happens that makes the difference in our lives. Your explanatory style definitely impacts the significant events in your life.

EEC

You can give the EEC test to your trading. Let the first E stand for the event. Something happens: that's the **event** and it creates its own reality. Let the second E stand for the **explanation** you give to the event. This explanation becomes your belief about the meaning and importance of the event. Let the C stand for the **consequences of the explanation** you gave the event. The consequences will be the actions you take in the future based on the belief engendered by the explanation. Let's look at some possible examples.

EVENT: You lost money on a trade.
EXPLANATION: Just the cost of doing business.
CONSEQUENCE: You take the next trade your methods offer you.

EVENT: You lost money on a trade.
EXPLANATION: It's impossible to make money in this market.
CONSEQUENCE: You skip the next trade which turns out to be a winner.

EVENT: You lost money on a trade.
EXPLANATION: If I don't make money, I'll be a loser. I'll lose my self-esteem.
CONSEQUENCE: You force the next trade and dig the losing hole deeper.

EVENT: You lost money on a trade.
EXPLANATION: The probabilities are that the next trade or the next will be a big winner.
CONSEQUENCE: You keep following your methods until you finally become profitable.

How you frame the event also has an effect upon the explanation and the consequence. In the above examples we simply said you lost money on a trade. That could have been broken down into more specific descriptions. For example: You hesitated and then chased a trade. You took a random trade. You didn't get out when your methods told you to, and a winner turned into a loser. You listened to your broker instead of following your methods. Each of these event descriptions would call forth a different kind of explanation. Let's take the first one as an example.

EVENT: You hesitated and then chased a trade.
EXPLANATION: It's dangerous to trade.

CONSEQUENCE: you stop trading and sit there frozen.

**EVENT: You hesitated and then chased a trade.
EXPLANATION: It's important to take a signal immediately.
CONSEQUENCE: You take the signals immediately.**

EVENT: **You hesitated and then chased a trade.**
EXPLANATION: **If you don't get into a trade right at the beginning, it's too late.**
CONSEQUENCE: **You sit there while the market is steaming up or down and you say it's too late now and miss the entire move.**

EVENT: **You hesitated and then chased a trade.**
EXPLANATION: **If you're late getting into a trade, you better use a fairly tight stop.**
CONSEQUENCE: **If it looks like there's more movement ahead, you enter, and you use a close stop.**

Examine your trading from the EEC viewpoint. Look at several important or recent events. Phrase each event with an accurate description. Explore your explanation. Note what are the likely consequences of your actions in response to the description and the explanation. Keep records in your trading notebook.

If you are a pessimist about your trading, you can train yourself to become an optimist by setting goals and creating positive expectations and bright pictures of your future. You can develop an explanatory style that supports you in what you want to do and be. What would it be like if you could be optimistic about your trading and your life as well?

1 *Learned Optimism,* **Martin E. P. Seligman, Ph.D., Alfred A. Knopf, 1991.**

Chapter 10

The Habitude of Open Mindedness and Clarity of Thought and Perception

"Why sometimes I've believed as many as six impossible things before breakfast."
—Lewis Carroll

"If a man will begin with certainties, he shall end in doubts; but if he will be content to begin with doubts, he shall end in certainties."
—Francis Bacon

The successful trader is open-minded. He is willing to take on information that is difficult to accept but which is factual, nonetheless. He is flexible and willing to shift course at a moment's notice. He stops telling himself stories that don't square with price action. He maintains an attitude of acceptance. He is willing to want what the market wants.

Such an attitude toward market action seems like a normal given. It's logical. But it's not the normal human condition. As humans, our perceptual apparatus necessarily deletes, distorts, and generalizes. We do this in order to build our models of the world. And then we reinforce our models of the world through more deletion, distortion, and generalization. We interpret our perceptions—that information we receive through our five senses—in the light of our past experiences. And we do that again and again. We create a bias.

The Problem of Bias

"A lively, disinterested, persistent liking for truth is extraordinarily rare."
—Henri Amiel

We all have multiple biases. We are Republicans. We are Democrats. We are conservative. We are liberal. We are Catholics. We are Baptists. We are Jews. We are vegetarians. We are meat eaters. We are optimists. We are pessimists. We are idealists. We are pragmatists. We have certain settled principles. We no longer examine those principles. Those formed values are the tracks on which we run our lives.

For the most part it works for us. We don't have to get up each morning and rethink our beliefs. There is a predictability of our model of the world. The mind is economic in its efforts. We can't keep rethinking everything. We'd never get anywhere. We put things into categories and into patterns. New information that comes in is simply altered and put into those preset arrangements.

A Matter of Identity

It goes even further than simple economy of thought. We resist changing our biases because they have become our identity. Our survival is hooked to our identity. Our identity is attached to our beliefs, our loyalties, and our history. Once we have identified ourself as a certain kind of thinker, believer, or person who behaves in a certain way, we will not easily let go of that. That is simply who we are. That is simply the way it is.

Bias in Trading Equals Danger

"What can we know, or what can we discern. When error chokes the windows of the mind?"
—**Sir John Davies**

Bias may work in the normal day to day activity, but when we take it into trading, we are endangered. The most expensive attitude you can have in trading is a closed mind. It will cost you money over and over again.

Some traders have a bullish bias. They're always thinking markets are going up, continuing to go up, or just about to go up. Others have a bearish bias. They love to short what they consider to be tops and love to sell into a sell off even when it may already be spent.

Some traders have a seasonal bias. For example, they anticipate the stock market will run up at the end of every year. Or that the stock market will collapse in September and October. Others like to buy orange juice in early winter in anticipation of a freeze. To be sure, history supports them to a considerable degree, but is it happening *now?*

Other traders have a predisposition to certain markets. I remember when gold was advancing towards $850, many were certain that it would go to $1,000. The Aden sisters said it would go to $4,000, and many believed them.

That takes us to the guru bias. Some traders will see evidence where none exists, that what their favorite prognosti-cator has said is starting to happen or will happen.

Others have a scenario bias. They've told themselves stories or listened to the stories others have told. The story has them mesmerized into believing that it's already happening or just about to take place.

How much money would you make if you could keep your natural biases from effecting your trading?

SOME WORDS AS CLUES

As you think about your trading, think about these words, and see if any of them has at some time applied to your trading: *inclination, bent, propensity, predilection, partiality, penchant, predisposition, attachment, proneness, leaning, fondness, disposition,liking,preference,susceptibility,weakness, proclivity, drift, slant, impulse, attraction, desire, whim, idio-*

syncrasy, persuasion, swayed, convinced, cajoled, or just plain certain.

Or maybe you have a negative bias. Think about these words, and see if they apply to your trading: *aversion, disinclination, distaste, distrust, dislike, doubt, unconvinced, rejection, disenchanted, disillusioned, disgusted, or just plain don't believe it.*

INDICATORS AS LIE DETECTORS

You need to develop some impartial indicator that will let you know whether or not your bias—your hunch—is in fact occurring. You need to create an unbiased set of rules for telling you whether a market is trending and what that trend is. And you need to pay attention to that indicator and factor it into your calculations. You could call it your no-nonsense detector. Keep asking yourself, "What is my no-nonsense detector telling me now?"

Certain questions can help us be alert to market action. "What is the market showing me now?" "What is the market telling me now?" "What do I feel in my bones the market is doing?" "Is there a clear trend?" "What is the trend?" 'Where is the opportunity on the long side?" "Where is the opportunity on the short side?" "Is there anything I'm not noticing?" "What would I think if I weren't in this trade?" "What does the price tell me?" "Are there lower highs and lows or are there higher lows and highs?" "Is price in a neutral range?"

The market gives us immediate and long term feedback. Feedback tells us if what we are doing is working or not. As traders we need to keep our perceptions clear so that we can respond to the feedback.

Sometimes a trader becomes so fearful of failure that he distorts or denies the accuracy of the feedback. Feedback is not failure, and it never has been. Feedback is simply information that what we are doing is working or not working. If what we are doing is not working, we need to do something else—soon.

As traders we need to long for the truth. We need to be buddies with the unadulterated facts. Of course, what is true now may not be true a minute from now. We are on an express train into the future. Unfortunately, we can only act in the now. Therefore, we need to see clearly, think clearly, and act decisively—NOW!

Chapter 11

The Habitude of Courage

"Courage is fear that said its prayers." —American Proverb

Courage is not recklessness, and it's not confident ease. It is a stepping up to do what needs to be done regardless of the possible negative consequences. If you know how to do it, and the results are certain to be positive, you don't need courage. Since there are no sure things in trading, and since loss is always a possibility, it takes courage to trade.

Practicing Courage

The good news is that courage can become a habit. The more you exercise courage in your trading, the easier it is to be courageous. As Thomas Jefferson said, **"The more you do, the more you can do."** Or as William Shakespeare said, *"Act **the part and become the part**,"* Ask yourself, "How would I trade if I were already courageous?"

Strangely enough, when things are difficult or challenging, we become stronger and happier. Watch when people become excited about something and their eyes are shining, they're often talking about a difficult challenge or an adversity overcome. They might be speaking about their first marathon run, a challenging tennis tournament, a speech in front of a large audience, a tough day's trading, or a business turn around.

We talked before about the word *flow* coined by Mihaly Csikszentmihalyi. Flow is the experience where a person is creating new responses to new challenges. To be in a state of flow, one needs to be challenged, but not too much. For example, you play cards with someone who is better than you, but not so much better that you can't compete. The rate of challenge never becomes so great that it's beyond a person's knowledge or skills, but the challenge is right at the edge of ability where the person is on her toes and totally and deeply absorbed.

If trading seems overwhelming to you, adjust your trading size downward until it's comfortable for you. If trading a one minute or five minute chart intraday has you at your wit's end, move to a larger time frame. Give yourself some breathing room. You want to be challenged but not over challenged. There's nothing wrong with taking baby steps before you take long strides.

Courageous Questions

Trading, indeed all of thinking, is about asking questions. Sometimes it takes courage to ask the right questions. "Is my trading profitable?" "Is what I'm doing working?" "Am I up or down on the year?" "Is there something I'd rather be doing?" "Could I make more money doing something else?" "Am I getting better at what I do?" "Do I need mentoring or coaching?"

Many years ago the President of Ford Motor Company had the courage to ask some significant questions. He asked his chief designer, "Do you like the cars you design?" The designer answered, "Well, frankly, no." The President had the courage to ask the designer to design a car he would like. The designer took him at his word and designed the Ford Thunderbird. The rest is history.

Walt Disney also had the courage to ask input from his whole company. He would story board a new movie and write above it, "How can we improve this?" The employees would respond and Walt Disney would take the input and make the changes essential to better the movie.

No courageous questions, no outstanding results. What is the question you need to ask to make your trading better?

Now, keep in mind there are questions that propel you forward and questions that debilitate. "Why am I such a loser?" is a question that can take you nowhere you want to go. First, it assumes that you are a loser and answering the why only convinces you further. "What's the matter with me?" is another question that will take you down a dead end alley. Much better to ask, "How can I become a winner?" "How can I become a wiser, stronger, more adventurous trader?"

RESPECT: NOT RECKLESSNESS

Courage does not mean recklessness. Successful traders have a deferential regard for the power of the market. They respect the potential force of current and future market moves. They realize that even when a market is moving back and forth lazily in a range, it can burst out of the range in a moment's notice. They respect the possibility of a trend to go and go and go—and also to reverse abruptly. They are prepared mentally for the unexpected because the unexpected often occurs. Just as a sailor respects the force of weather and tides, so the successful trader respects the hidden and apparent force of the market.

Respect applies to all aspects of trading. Live orders are viewed as live ammunition and are treated accordingly. Orders are checked and rechecked. Stop loss orders are cancelled immediately after a trade is finished. Resting orders are also reviewed to be certain they are current.

Successful traders have respect for their capital. They know what it can do for them and for others. They know how hard they worked to create it and to grow it. They do not treat their capital as easy come, easy go. They value it.

Successful traders have respect for their verified methods. If their method tells them the market is going down, they believe it, and abide by it. If their method tells them it's time to enter the market, they do it promptly. If their method tells them to exit a trade, they do it. Because of their respect for their method, they allow it to guide them. They would not dare trade on the opposite side of their methods.

No. Courage is not foolhardiness. You know what they say about pilots. There are old pilots and bold pilots, but there are no old, bold pilots. The same is true of traders. The old, bold trader has lost his capital. In trading courage is a careful walk in the face of uncertainty. Trading is a brave, open-minded walk through what often appears to be chaotic conditions. That is why successful traders respect the unknown and take advantage of insurance mechanisms such as risk management and money management to protect themselves.

The Hero's Journey

It has been said that each of us is on a hero's journey. According to Joseph Campbell,[1] myths of many cultures relate the story of a hero's journey. We can look at the myth of a hero's journey as a metaphor for our own journey on our life's path. Myths are to cultures as dreams are to individuals. According to Campbell, the journey is composed of a series of steps.

First, there is the calling. The calling relates to our identity, life purpose or mission. We can choose to either accept or ignore the calling. *When did you first hear your calling to trade, to enter an arena rich with rewards and corrections?*

Second, we accept the calling. This leads us to confront a boundary or threshold in our existing abilities or perception of life and the world. *Remember when you first began to trade and stepped into this arena where you needed new abilities and perceptions.*

Third, crossing the threshold thrusts us into some new life territory, and it forces us to grow and evolve. We need to find support and guidance. *How did you evolve in your trading? Where did you first look to find support and guidance?*

Fourth, finding a guardian or mentor is something that often comes naturally from having the courage to cross a threshold. Remember the saying that when the student is ready, the teacher appears. *What mentors and coaches have appeared to assist you in your development as a trader?*

Fifth, facing a challenge (or "demon") is also a natural result of having crossed the threshold. These "demons" are not necessarily evil or bad. They represent a type of energy or power that we need to learn to deal with. Often they are a reflection of our own inner shadows or weaknesses. *What "demons" have you confronted in your trading? How have you contended with them? How have you accepted them?*

Sixth, as heroes we transform the "demon" into a resource or advisor. We develop special skills. We discover special resources or tools. *How have you transformed your limitations in trading into skills and strengths? What personal resources have you brought to bear on the issue? What tools assist you to overcome the inherent weaknesses in the process of your trading?*

Seventh, finding the way to fulfill the calling is ultimately achieved by creating an inner map or interpretation of the world that incorporates the growth and discoveries brought about by the journey. *What new descriptions of life and trading have resulted from your journey into trading?*

Eighth, we return home as a transformed or evolved person. *In what ways has trading helped you to evolve as a trader and a person? In what ways would you like to keep evolving?*

Yes, as a trader you are on a hero's journey. Each trading day is part of that journey. Each day you bring your courage to the day's trading, and each day you become wiser and more powerful. As J. M. Barrie says, *"Courage is the thing. All goes if courage goes."* You maintain your courage.

[1] *The Power of Myth*, Joseph Campbell, 1988.

Chapter 12

The Habitude of Discipline

"Diligence is the mother of good luck."
—Benjamin Franklin

Discipline is one of those words that evokes going to the principal's office or facing an angry father when he comes home. We think of discipline and we think of punishment, limits, and curbs. We may even think of outside unbending authoritarian control.

The original use of the word discipline involved the education or training of disciples. Later the word came to include control.

Education and Control of the Self

When I speak of discipline in trading, I'm talking about self-discipline. I'm talking about both education and control of the self. I'm talking about self-chosen disciplined designs for trading. I'm talking about disciplined limits and actions imposed by the self.

People resist discipline including self-discipline. When I ask my clients to write down their trading rules, some object. They don't like rules and authoritarian constraints. "Okay," I say, "write down a set of guidelines or principles for clarity of action."

To some people, discipline is doing what you don't want to do. For me, discipline is doing whatever needs to be done to achieve your goals. If your goal is a healthy, trim body, that means healthy eating, exercise, and sufficient sleep. If your goal is wealth, then there are certain actions you need to take in relation to spending, saving, investing, and trading. There are no short cuts to these results. You do what needs to be done *whether or not you feel like it.*

Trading With Integrity

Disciplined trading means trading with integrity. For me, integrity is being what you say you are, and doing what you say you'll do. To trade with integrity you need clean and speedy data, verified indicators and methods that give you an edge, sufficient capital, and a mind-set that supports trading. Successful traders discipline themselves through mental training to do what will most probably work.

Many traders are willing to spend plenty of time and money on systems development, but unwilling to spend time and money on their own self-development. This is understandable in that it's natural to deny that there's anything remiss about oneself. The answer, they think—or so the ads would convince us—lies out there in some magnificent system, some "holy grail."

A system, no matter how good, is not enough because it is administered by a trader. That trader's personal mental control and flexibility has a multiplier effect upon any system's results. **There are no short cuts around the trading self.**

Successful traders have schooled their minds to think clearly and act in concert with their thinking and their methods regardless of how they may feel. Discipline means cutting your losses and letting your profits run. It means trading in the right size—not too much and not too little. It means acting in a timely fashion, making a decision and acting upon that decision at the right time. You can't jump the gun, and you can't wait too long. It means doing your homework and being prepared. It means doing what you say you're going to do, and being who you say you are.

Trading discipline involves integrity of thought and action. If I have a goal, then my actions support that goal. If I don't act upon my goal, then I'm just wishing. Successful traders know what needs to be done, and they do it. No excuses. No evasions. Simple, clean thought and action.

Doing Not Trying

"If at first you don't succeed, try, try again." —*proverb*

We all grew up with the proverb. Try and try until you succeed. And it seemed like wholesome, good advice. But I would submit that trying has a negative component. Let me ask you this. Are you *trying* to stop over trading your account? Are you *trying* to stop hesitating before entering a trade? Are you *trying* to stop fighting your way out of losing trades instead of just getting out? Are you *trying* to follow your trading rules?

It comes down to this. If you're trying, you're not succeeding. When somebody tells you that they'll try to get to your party, you know they won't come. I remember once a motivational speaker asked a member of the audience to try and pick up a bunch of papers. When the person picked them up, the speaker said, "No. Don't pick them up. Try and pick them up." Finally the audience member placed his hands on the papers and pretended to try unsuccessfully to pick up the papers.

Remember the children's story about the little engine that could? The engine said, "I think I can. I think I can." Finally, the little engine said, "I thought I could. I thought I could." Success came to the little engine who took action. It wasn't a story about the little engine that tried.

What is it about trying that seems to work against us? The first definition of the Oxford American Dictionary for try is to attempt, to make an effort to do something. Perhaps effort or attempt does not contemplate success but rather struggle.

One of my clients reported to me that he used to try very hard not to get stuck in losing trades, not to fight against the market. And yet he invariably would from time to time refuse to take off a losing trade and find himself fighting against his very own indicators struggling not to have a losing trade or a losing day. He'd dig the hole deeper and deeper and end up the "failure" he didn't want to be. Now, he says he's not trying, and he's not getting stuck. He's succeeding.

Through our work something shifted for this client. His intentions changed. His confidence level rose. His beliefs changed. His perceptions altered. His automatic response to a losing trade or losing day was different. He interpreted a losing trade or day as simply that. No big deal. He was still the competent trader who would go on to win.

The little engine that could had confidence in its ability to get to the top of the hill. It intended to succeed. It perceived the uphill journey as an adventure of possibility.

If you're trying to do or not do something in your trading and you're not succeeding, you need to shift something. Ask yourself, "What would I need to believe in order to do or not do this?" "How would I have to interpret this event in order to handle it differently?" "What are my real underlying intentions in regard to this situation?" "How would I have to feel about myself in order to succeed at this?"

If you're trying and not succeeding in some aspect of your trading, don't try, try again. Do something different. Discipline is doing, not trying. Change your interpretations. Modify a belief. Alter your guidelines. Allow yourself to feel differently about the consequences of the behavior you're trying to do or not to do. What if you can become the little trader that can? What if you can become the big trader that could?

ACTING IN SUPPORT OF TRADING GOALS

Set down in writing your trading goals. What do you need to do to achieve these goals? What skills do you need to acquire? What do you need to believe? What resources do you need in order to do this? List a set of actions that will help you get to your goals. Set a time table for yourself. See it accomplished out there in your future.

SPECIFIC TRADING GUIDELINES

While you're at it, write out a set of trading rules for yourself. Write your rules for entry and your rules for exit— with a profit and with a loss. You can also write a set of rules for telling yourself whether or not a market is trending and what that trend is. Watch to see how clearly you adhere to your rules. If you can't adhere to your trading rules, your guidelines, then you know you need mental coaching. It's not a lost cause. There are state of the art techniques for acquiring a mental toughness and a clear will to win. I work every day with traders to install a winning discipline.

TRADING AS AN ART AND ADVENTURE

Keep in mind that trading with discipline is more than simply adhering to a set of rules. Trading is an art as well as a discipline. It is an art to pick a set of guiding principles and an art to know when to strictly apply them and when to suspend them. Trading is an artful discipline and a disciplined art.

Trading is also an adventure filled with surprises—some delightful and some startling. Successful traders love the process of trading. And they bring to the process a disciplined adventurousness and an adventurous discipline. They trade with both heart and mind.

Balance

Superb trading is balanced. The twelve habitudes of highly successful traders all work together to provide a winning balance. Each habitude enhances and modifies the others. For example, we have detached preparation and prepared detachment. We have courageous open-mindedness and open-minded courage. We have risk taking optimism and optimistic risk taking. We have disciplined abundance consciousness and abundant thinking discipline.

Also each of the habitudes applies to itself to intensify itself. For example, we have detached detachment, willing willingness to accept loss, risk taking acceptance of risk, probabilities thinking assessment of probabilities, optimistic optimism, open-minded open-mindedness, courageous courage, and, of course, disciplined discipline.

Highly successful trading is a holistic blend of many habitual attitudes. It is a balanced trading combining desire and caution, equanimity and power, heart and head, art and science, adventure and discipline. Let these attitudes and approaches to trading become your habits of mind. And do it with heart.

Biography

Ruth Barrons Roosevelt coaches traders around the world to trading excellence. She is exceptionally well qualified to offer such guidance to traders, as she herself has extensive trading experience and is to this day an active trader. Her experience covers multiple time frames, from position trading in virtually every futures market, to active and intense intraday trading in currencies, T-bonds, and S&P futures. She has traded S&P's extensively and actively since inception of trading in 1984, down to and including 1 minute bars. Her trading experience also includes active trading of mutual funds and equities.

She is a former Vice President of **Prudential Securities** and of **Thomson** McKinnon. From 1981to 1986 she headed the **International Moneyline** trading desk at **Rudolf Wolf** (New York). Before that she was a stock and futures broker at **Drexel Burnham Lambert** where she broke records by opening 250 accounts in one month. A graduate of the **University of Michigan Law School,** she is a member of the New York and California Bar Association. A frequent contributor to *Technical Analysis of Stocks and Commodities,* she writes articles on the psychology of successful trading. She is the coauthor of *Living In Step* **(McGraw Hill,** 1976). As founder and director of The **Wall Street Hypnosis Center,** she works with Wall Street professionals to achieve their optimal effectiveness.

Ruth has appeared on numerous national and international television programs including: **CBS, NBC, CNN,** and **WWOR Evening News, CNBC, NBC The Today Show, Good Morning American, Japan Public Television, Nippon Television, Hungarian Public Television, Finland Television Channel 3,** and the **David Letterman Late Night Show.**

She has been profiled for her work with traders in *Business Week, Barron's, The New York Times, New York Magazine, The Independent* of London, *The Toronto Star,* and many other publications.

Ruth has written four more books on trading psychology. They are Exceptional Trading: The Mind Game, Overcoming Seven Deadly Sins of Trading, Keeping a Cool Head in a Hot Market, and Mind Power: Thought Techniques for High-Powered Trading.

ADDITIONAL BOOKS BY RUTH BARRONS ROOSEVELT

Exceptional Trading: The Mind Game

"True to its title, Ruth has done an exceptional job. Her explanations are clear and concise, but most of all, I think some of her techniques are brilliant. Thanks for sharing, Ruth. This book is a real credit to the industry."
Mark Douglas

Overcoming 7 Deadly Sins Of Trading

Technical analysis of markets is, to a degree, a graphical depiction of
The interplay between bullish and bearish market participants.
Underlying their trading decisions is a wide range of emotions, as well as good and bad trading habits and attitudes. Ruth Roosevelt's book does a marvelous job of showing the reader how to understand these emotions, habits, and attitudes, and how to use them to advantage in arriving at effective trading decisions."
John Murphy, World Renowned Technical Analyst and Author

KEEPING A COOL HEAD IN A HOT MARKET

This book will help you keep the balance between risk and reward, between protecting your capital and growing your capital. The crucial enigma at the core of trading is taking advantage of market opportunities while preserving the source and medium of your trading and investing.

Mind Power: Thought Techniques for High-Powered Trading

The human mind is a powerful engine for success— or failure.

How you run your mental machinery is crucial to your profitability as a trader or investor. This book has 64 separate steps and explorations that you can use one at a time to become the trader you dream of being.